Bluegrass

The Life, Times & Music® Series

Bluegrass

The Life, Times & Music® Series

Chris Seymour

FRIEDMAN/FAIRFAX

PUBLISHERS

ISBN 1-56799-355-9

Editor: Stephen Slaybaugh
Art Director: Lynne Yeamans
Designer: Galen Smith
Photography Editor: Kathryn Culley
Production Manager: Jeanne E. Hutter

Grateful acknowledgment is given to authors, publishers, and photographers for permission to reprint material. Every effort has been made to determine copyright owners of photographs and illustrations. In the case of any omissions, the publishers will be pleased to make suitable acknowledgments in future editions.

Color separations by HK Scanner Arts Int'l Ltd.
Printed in Hong Kong and bound in China by Midas Printing Limited

For bulk purchases and special sales, please contact:
Friedman/Fairfax Publishers
Attention: Sales Department
15 West 26th Street
New York, New York 10010
212/685-6610   FAX 212/685-1307

Visit the Friedman/Fairfax Website:
http://www.webcom.com/friedman

Front Cover Photography Credits:
Background: FPG International/© Ron Thomas
Bill Monroe: UPI/Corbis-Bettmann
Flatt, Scruggs and The Foggy Mountain Boys: Frank Driggs Collection

Acknowledgments

This book would not have been written without the help of numerous people who gave selflessly of their time to respond to multiple requests for information, including: Mary Armstrong, Katie Blankenship of *Bluegrass Unlimited*, Frank Godbey, Steve Goldfield, Kent Henderson of the Country Music Foundation, Murphy Henry, Bruce Kallick, John Lupton of Brandywine Friends of Old-Time Music, James Reams, Gary Reid, and Ron Thomason.

I am also grateful to Rebekah Radisch of Sugar Hill Records, Glen Dicker and Terry Kitchen of Rounder Records, and Tor Elting of Flying Fish Records, who provided recordings of numerous bluegrass artists on short notice.

This short book scratches the surface of the story of bluegrass and leans heavily on the work of historians and analysts who have told the story in greater depth, most notably Bill Malone, Robert Cantwell, and especially Neil Rosenberg. Readers who want to explore the subject more deeply will find, as I did, their excellent books most helpful.

My editor, Steve Slaybaugh, helped clarify my prose and was a pleasure to work with.

Finally, I am deeply indebted to my comrade, best friend and partner-in-crime, Judith Mahoney Pasternak, who reviewed the manuscript at several stages and offered the perfect mix of encouragement, criticism, and substantive editorial comment.

Dedication

For my parents, Mary Hale Meyer and Evan Seymour, who encouraged me to sing and play music, and taught me to love words.

Contents

Introduction

A round the middle of the twentieth century, artists playing a

new breed of music exploded onto the American scene,

wowing audiences and inspiring dozens of bands to re-

shape their sound. This music drew heavily on the blues

and was punctuated by infectious African-American rhythms.

This new music was bluegrass, which predated

rock and roll by about five years.

When people hear bluegrass for the first time, most assume that it's as old as the hills, yet it's actually younger than bebop. Bluegrass—at least traditional bluegrass—does sound old. It is played on acoustic instruments; many of the songs have old-fashioned themes, such as the loss of beloved parents or exile

Opposite: Bluegrass grew out of homemade rural music. Below: Bill (left) and Charlie Monroe had a stormy musical partnership that started in their youth on their father's Kentucky farm.

from the old home place; and its roots in rural southern music, white and black, are certainly old. But when founding figures like mandolinist Bill Monroe (b. 1911) and banjo player Earl Scruggs (b. 1924) grafted high-voltage instrumental improvisation (from jazz) onto those roots, they created a form that has spawned both further musical innovation and exploration of the rural southern tradition, keeping bluegrass' musical roots fresh and vital.

Bluegrass Roots

Although the bluegrass audience and musicians are almost exclusively white, the origins of bluegrass music are as much African-American as they are European-American. Its immediate sources are the blues; "hillbilly" music of the 1920s and 1930s, which was much more racially mixed than is usually acknowledged and which owes much to blackface minstrels' appropriations of black music; and Dixieland jazz.

Blues guitarist Brownie McGhee (right) taught A.P. Carter songs that then entered the (white) country repertoire.

The Carter Family—Maybelle (left), brother in law, A.P., and cousin, Sara, A.P.'s wife—collected or wrote dozens of songs that became bluegrass standards.

When a parade of record company talent scouts, led by Okeh's Ralph Peer, headed into the rural South in search of new "product" in the 1920s, they put the music they found into two neat categories: "hillbilly" music—songs and dance tunes by and for white people—and "race" music—blues and spirituals by and for black people. In real life, as opposed to record catalogs, rural southern music was not so strictly segregated. There was a common repertoire of songs played by both black and white musicians, from ballads ("Casey Jones," "John Henry") to party songs ("Mama Don't 'low," "Salty Dog") to sacred songs ("Oh Mary Don't You Weep," "Old Time Religion"). And although the scouts missed most of them, there were numerous black string bands that played for both black and white dances. This is not surprising, given that the dance bands—black and white—were playing an amalgamation of the jigs and

The blues of Jimmie Rodgers, country's first superstar, were all over the airwaves in the late twenties and early thirties and heavily influenced bluegrass founder Bill Monroe.

reels brought over from Ireland and Scotland (represented by the fiddle) and African rhythms and melodies (represented by the banjo). One black square dance band that the scouts did find, the Mississippi Sheiks, ended up on Columbia's list of "old-time" (white) recordings. Meanwhile, plenty of white performers took up the blues. Jimmie Rodgers (1897–1933), the blue yodeler, was only the most famous example. Banjo player Dock Boggs (1898–1971), a Virginia coal miner, was another. He learned "Mistreated Mama Blues" and "Down South Blues," among others, from black musicians and recorded them for Brunswick in the late 1920s.

A.P. Carter (1891–1960) collected numerous songs from black blues guitarist Brownie McGhee (b. 1915). (Carter was one of the famous Carter Family, who, along with Rodgers, were recorded in Peer's landmark 1927 Bristol, Tennessee, sessions that launched the hillbilly recording trend.) The distinctive guitar style of Maybelle Carter (1909–1978), in which melody notes picked out on the bass strings are punctuated by rhythmic brushes across all the strings, was probably influenced by black guitarist Leslie Riddle (1905–1980), whom the Carters took with them on their song-collecting trips. Maybelle's style, dubbed the "Carter scratch," would in turn influence bluegrass guitarists such as Lester Flatt (1914–1979).

Bill Monroe

The blues became infused into the music that would become bluegrass largely because of Bill Monroe. A shy, nearsighted outsider as a child, Monroe defied convention among whites in his hometown, Rosine, Kentucky, when he sought out a black musician, Arnold Schultz (d. 1931), as his mentor. Schultz was a blues guitarist and fiddler who mined coal by day and played at local dances by

As a youth, Bill Monroe sought out musicians on the margins of rural Rosine society, including his shack-dwelling bachelor uncle, fiddler Pen Vandiver, and black blues musician Arnold Schultz.

The Banjo

His long day in the fields done, the slave picks up a gourd drum that has a long wooden neck and starts hitting at the strings that stretch the length of the instrument. A haunting, mournful air emerges. Then a driving, syncopated tune sets feet tapping throughout the compound and catches the ear of the master's son passing by.

The long-necked strung gourd was called the *mbanza* in the slave's West African home. Today, it is the banjo, played almost exclusively by whites, and it defines bluegrass in the popular imagination.

Not long after the establishment of plantation culture, masters began putting slaves to work making music for dancing. The slave bands played European instruments, such as the violin, but they kept the banjo, playing it in the style that came to be called "frailing" or "clawhammer," in which the player's hand, curled into a claw shape, strikes strings individually or in a strum—always on a downstroke—with the back of a fingernail.

White musicians started learning—and later parodying—this plantation music in the early nineteenth century. Their blackface minstrel shows featured the banjo, played clawhammer at first and later in a three-finger style that presaged ragtime. Black performers—in blackface—started treading the minstrel floorboards after Emancipation, often as banjo virtuosos. It was probably they who evolved this more melodic banjo method to play the more complex popular songs that composers such as Stephen Foster were writing for the minstrel stage. The banjo remained fretless until the 1880s, when manufacturers such as the S.S. Stewart Company started mass-producing the instrument and added frets for greater ease of playing.

The minstrel banjo player was usually a comic figure, a stereotyped buffoon, an image that has clung to the banjo. Around the turn of the century, black musicians started to leave the banjo behind, taking up the guitar, which was trickling down from its recent vogue in the parlors of the middle class in cities around the country. The banjo persisted in the string bands that played for Saturday night dances in the hills and hollows of Appalachia. The three-finger style endured, particularly in western North Carolina, where Charlie Poole and his North Carolina Ramblers and then Snuffy Jenkins and his Jenkins' String Band featured the style in their popular bands.

Jenkins had developed a way of playing syncopated three-finger "banjo rolls" around the melody that grabbed the attention of his listeners on WIS in Columbia, South Carolina, in the 1930s. Two of them, Earl Scruggs and Don Reno, would take the technique to another level and introduce it to the world with Bill Monroe and his Blue Grass Boys in the 1940s. By the 1970s, the banjo was everywhere, featured on soundtracks for *Bonnie and Clyde*, *Deliverance*, and *The Beverly Hillbillies* as well as seemingly half the television commercials of the period. Today the drum with strings is a central component of the bluegrass sound.

White minstrels blackened their faces and appropriated African-Americans' music, including their instruments, namely the banjo.

night. Monroe played backup at some of those dances in his teens, and Schultz's playing had a heavy impact on the young musician: it instilled in him an abiding love for the blues that emerges in many of his songs, including the first mandolin tune he wrote, "Tennessee Blues," and in the use of the blues scale in countless bluegrass numbers.

Bill was the youngest of six children born on a western Kentucky farm,

and his mother, born Malissa Vandiver, was his first musical influence. She played fiddle, harmonica, and accordion and sang, inculcating a love for music in her son before she died when he was ten years old. His older brothers, Birch (1901–1982) and Charlie (1903–1975), dictated Bill's choice of instrument. They wouldn't let him play guitar or fiddle but forced him onto the mandolin, which then was used almost exclusively for backup. The mandolin became the channel for all of Bill's frustrations. Although he dutifully played rhythm for the family's musical gatherings—and for his uncle, Pendleton Vandiver, a fiddler at local dances, as well as Shultz— he also began developing the mandolin as a lead instrument.

Bill wanted to make the mandolin sing like his uncle Pen's fiddle, but with some of the blues sound he was hearing from Schultz and other black singers and musicians who worked as laborers in the area. He also listened carefully to Rodgers'

In the early 1930s, Bill and Charlie Monroe worked as exhibition square dancers in the cast of the WLS National Barn Dance, the nation's first big country music showcase.

white blues, which were then taking the southern airwaves by storm. Monroe eventually developed a complex, driving, yet sensitive sound that revolution-ized the way that the mandolin is played.

Too nearsighted to play baseball with other boys his age, Monroe spent many an afternoon in the fields singing to himself. There he developed his high, mournful holler, styled after the "shouting" singing style of black field hands. Monroe's voice as much as his mandolin has helped define the "high lonesome" sound that prompted Ron Thomason (b. 1944) of the band Dry Branch Fire Squad to observe: "Lonesome is to bluegrass music as blue is to the blues."

When Bill was sixteen years old, his seventy-year-old father died, so he went to live with his uncle Pen. But life was fairly rough in the one-room cabin with Vandiver, a widower and something of an outsider himself, so Bill left Rosine and joined his siblings in East Chicago, Indiana, in 1929. The Depression had hit the rural South long before the stock market crash, and his two brothers had gone north to look for work. Bill got a day job at the Sinclair oil refinery and worked there through the early 1930s, sometimes supporting his brothers when they were out of work. Nights and weekends, Birch, Charlie, and Bill worked as a trio at dances and on local radio stations. Then they got hired as exhibition dancers with the touring unit of Chicago's WLS National Barn Dance, which was the country's premier hillbilly music program.

The rise of industry and the crash of the farm economy actually helped create country music. The two phenomena had brought tens of thousands of people like the Monroes from farms in Tennessee, Kentucky, and elsewhere to the grim manufacturing cities in Illinois, Indiana, and Michigan. The mixing together of rural immigrants from different states helped break down regional musical styles, which had varied significantly from county to county, especially in the isolated Appalachian region. And the people's longing for songs about the romanticized old South only increased the appeal of hillbilly music with the transplants. The gathering of rural southerners in Chicago, East Chicago, Hammond, Gary, and nearby towns created a concentrated market for rural music. In addition, the Depression made regular work hard to find, and professional music-making became an attractive alternative.

Two of the Monroes didn't hesitate when the contacts they had made through WLS led to an opportunity in 1934 to say good-bye forever to the oil refinery. They received an offer to do a radio show in Shenandoah, Iowa. Birch wasn't ready to take the risk and stayed at Sinclair, but Charlie and Bill went on KFNF as the Monroe Brothers.

Higher and Faster than the Average Duet

There were numerous brother duets performing hillbilly music at the time who played guitar and mandolin and sang close harmonies. Both the Delmore Brothers and the Blue Sky Boys, for example, were quite popular. But Bill and Charlie Monroe's sound already had distinctive elements that would later be central to bluegrass. They sang in higher keys than most, with Bill's field-honed tenor harmony reaching for that high, lonesome sound that would become classic. Charlie's bass runs on guitar and Bill's intricate, blues-inflected mandolin work made for striking accompaniment. And they played faster than almost anybody, giving their music extra punch.

From 1934 to 1938 they moved from station to station—from Shennadoah to Omaha and then around the Carolinas—drawing their repertoire from Jimmie Rodgers, country's first solo singing star; the Carter Family; and string

Bill Monroe (seated) quarreled with his brother and formed his own band, the Blue Grass Boys, in 1938. By 1939 the quartet won a spot on WSM's Grand Ole Opry program in Nashville (opposite).

bands such as Mainer's Mountaineers and Gid Tanner and His Skillet Lickers. It was probably during this period that Bill heard iconoclastic fiddler Clayton McMichen (1900–1970), whom Bill cites as a major influence. McMichen played the hick with the Skillet Lickers, but he found the hillbilly role constricting; when he started his own band, the Georgia Wildcats, in 1931, he began playing jazz tunes like Benny Goodman's "Farewell Blues." His hot fiddling excited Monroe and other musicians but failed to catch on with southeastern audiences the way fiddler Bob Wills' western swing sound did in the southwest.

The Monroe Brothers were growing in popularity and attracting ever larger crowds. Starting in 1936, they recorded sixty songs for Bluebird, Victor's hillbilly label. In 1938, however, long-simmering tensions and rivalry between Bill and Charlie came to a head. Charlie, eight years Bill's senior, had always insisted on calling the shots, and his younger brother resented it. They quarreled and went their separate musical ways. Discussing or even referring to his work with Charlie has remained almost taboo with Bill Monroe to this day.

From Garage Band to Grand Ole Opry

Charlie, who had handled business for the duo, kept the recording contract and was initially more successful than his younger brother. Bill advertised in the newspapers and hired young singer and guitar player Cleo Davis, fiddler Art Wooten, and bass player/singer/comedian Amos Garen. Monroe parked his trailer in Greenville, North Carolina, behind a gas station, where he used a shed out back to rehearse his band. He called them the Blue Grass Boys, named for his home state. For a year and a half or so they played on small stations and for small audiences while they developed their sound.

The bass was one innovation. Country musicians were just starting to use the instrument, common in jazz, and it provided Monroe's band with the rhythmic grounding that allowed the players to stay together while playing at breakneck speed. Christian songs were a big part of the hillbilly repertoire—Bill and Charlie had done many of them—but the Blue Grass Boys added the rich harmony of the black and white gospel quartets popular in the South in the twenties and thirties. When the group did gospel numbers, they played only guitar and mandolin, and

SOUVENIR PROGRAM

THE GRAND OLE OPRY
THE MOTHER CHURCH OF COUNTRY MUSIC

Comedian Dave "Stringbean" Akeman was the first banjo player to play with the Blue Grass Boys.

renamed themselves the Blue Grass Quartet. Three- and four-part harmony on secular as well as sacred songs would evevtually become an important part of the bluegrass sound.

Spending their mornings on the radio, their afternoons rehearsing in the garage, and their evenings playing for small crowds at schoolhouses, the Blue Grass Boys developed into a cohesive unit. By the autumn of 1939, Monroe was ready to take them for a shot at the big time: the Grand Ole Opry.

The Opry, today the oldest continually aired radio show in the country and the anchor of the Opryland theme park, started in 1925 as an hourlong program of solo fiddle music. It was hosted by George D. Hay (1895–1968), a former journalist who had worked at WLS in Chicago and was trying to replicate the success of the WLS National Barn Dance on Nashville's brand-new station, WSM. Hay adopted the persona of the Solemn Old Judge, a role borrowed from his newspaper columns, which he wrote as dialogues between two minstrel-show stereotypes, a white judge and a black defendant. Hay's down-home manner and insistence on down-to-earth music attracted dozens of musicians and tens of thousands of listeners. When Monroe auditioned, the Grand Ole Opry—so named in 1927, when Hay took an on-air jab at the classical music program preceding his broadcast—was replacing the National Barn Dance as the number one hillbilly music program.

The Boys wowed the Judge with a vastly sped-up version of Rodgers' "Muleskinner Blues," which remains one of Monroe's trademark songs to this day. Hay told Monroe, "If you ever leave the Opry, it'll be because you've fired yourself." Broadcast on WSM's fifty thousand watts of clear-channel airwaves, the Opry exposed the band's evolving sound to a huge audience throughout eastern and central North America. When Davis, Wooten, and Garen each moved on, Monroe didn't have to advertise in the newspapers to find replacements; he had musicians knocking down his doors.

Is It Bluegrass Yet?

Several of the fiddlers who played with Monroe during the next several years would help establish the bluegrass fiddle sound, which was jazzier as well as faster than traditional old-time dance fiddling. Howdy Forrester (1922–1987), who joined the band in early 1942, had lived in Texas from 1939 to 1941 and was influenced by the western swing style that was

Blue Grass Boys guitarist/lead singer Lester Flatt thought Akeman's banjo playing slowed the band down.

burgeoning in the area. (He would later play with country great Roy Acuff [1903–1992].) Forrester's successor, Chubby Wise (1915–1996), writer of the future bluegrass cliché "Orange Blossom Special," also had a swing background. So did consummate bluegrass fiddler Kenny Baker (b. 1921), who would join Monroe in the late fifties/early sixties and again from 1968 through the mid-1980s. Baker lists jazz bandleaders Benny Goodman and Tommy Dorsey among his major influences.

In 1942, Monroe hired his first banjo player, Dave "Stringbean" Akeman (1914–1973), a step that would prove critical to the development of bluegrass. Stringbean used the two-finger, "clawhammer" style, and as was common for white banjo players of the era, he also did comedy skits in blackface.

By popular demand, WSM's Artists' Service Department began sending the band out on the Opry's tent-show tours. By 1943, Monroe was able to start his own show, buying a nine-passenger Packard limo with a roof rack for the bass and setting out with five trucks full of canvas and bleachers to barnstorm small towns around the South. The band often drummed up interest by fielding a baseball team to challenge local sluggers. Before wartime shellac shortages and a musicians'

Banjoist Earl Scruggs (left) blew away Monroe, Flatt (right), and Grand Ole Opry audiences when he joined the Blue Grass Boys.

union dispute stopped record production for several years, the Blue Grass Boys recorded a number of sides for Bluebird, including their showstopper, "Muleskinner Blues."

The year 1945 was crucial in the development of the music that nobody yet called bluegrass. First, guitarist and lead singer Lester Flatt joined the Blue Grass Boys. He wrote several songs with Monroe, blended seamless vocal harmonies with him, and played rock-solid rhythm guitar, ending phrases with the "Lester Flatt G-run," which has come to define bluegrass rhythm guitar. Flatt thought Stringbean's banjo slowed the band down, so he was pleased when

Flatt (second from left) and Scruggs (right), tired of Monroe calling all the shots, left the Blue Grass Boys to form their own band, the Foggy Mountain Boys (pictured here).

Akeman left, but still felt dubious about replacing him. After a brief attempt to import the popular hot jazz sound directly into his band·by hiring Dixieland-style four-string banjo player Jim Andrews, Monroe hired a banjo player who changed Flatt's mind—and music history.

Born on a farm near Flint Hill, North Carolina, Earl Scruggs played the three-finger banjo style common in the area. The way he played it, however, was anything but common. North Carolina string-band leaders like Charlie Poole (1892–1931) and Snuffy Jenkins (1908–1990), who were probably influenced by black ragtime banjo pickers, had played the banjo "guitar-style" in the 1920s, with thumb, forefinger, and middle finger. Scruggs took the technique to another level, picking out the melody and surrounding it with a shower of syncopated notes, and he was able to pick as fast as the Blue Grass Boys played.

Monroe hired Scruggs on the spot. He brought the house down at his first Opry performance, and the banjo became a defining element of bluegrass music. (Partisans of another banjo giant, Don Reno [1927–1984], point out that he almost had Scruggs' spot with the Blue Grass Boys. They say Monroe had

tried to hire Reno, also a Jenkins disciple and three-finger banjo innovator, the previous year, but Reno had to decline in favor of a governmental invitation to serve in the army.)

The three years Monroe, Flatt, and Scruggs were together were golden. Flatt wrote songs such as "Will You Be Loving Another Man?" and the band went to town on them, playing in a new jazz ensemble style with each instrument taking a solo break. In the backseat of the Packard on the way to gigs, the three would work out arrangements of old songs from Monroe's youth, like "Little Maggie," another bluegrass standard-to-be. The band would dazzle audiences with new material every night. Flatt, with his genial, casual stage presence, took on emcee duties for the group. Scruggs often soloed after every verse; audiences went wild over his banjo. The band recorded twenty-eight songs for Columbia in 1946 and 1947, although only a few were released while the three were still together. One was Monroe's "Blue Moon of Kentucky," a waltz that Elvis Presley (1935–1977) would later speed up and make into one of his early hits.

In 1948, tired of a grueling tour schedule and taking orders from Monroe, and wanting to earn the serious money they could make as bandleaders rather than as employees, Flatt and Scruggs left the Blue Grass Boys. With Blue Grass Boys alumni fiddler Jimmy Shumate and bassist Howard Watts (Cedric Rainwater), along with singer/guitarist Mac Wiseman (b. 1925), who would later play with Monroe, Flatt and Scruggs founded the Foggy Mountain Boys. That spring they went on the air in Bristol, Virginia, over WCYB, which would become the country's premier bluegrass station. Already well known, they generated sacks of fan mail and requests for personal appearances, drawing hundreds of fans to shows around the region.

Festivals: Bluegrass Camp Meetings

When the weather turns warm, bluegrass and its fans go camping.

The bluegrass calendar revolves around the summer ritual of festivals, as tens of thousands of fans, many of them musicians themselves, make pilgrimages to extended weekend gatherings. They come to hear old favorites and up-and-coming bands, jam in the campgrounds and parking lots, reconnect with friends from past years, and renew the true faith of bluegrass music. It's difficult to imagine that in 1961, promoter Bill Clifton's idea of devoting an entire day—let alone a whole weekend—to a bluegrass concert was a radical one.

Conventional wisdom then held that country music concerts should never include more than one bluegrass band: one was deemed enough to draw bluegrass fans, and adding others would supposedly draw no more. Nonetheless, Clifton rounded up many of bluegrass' leading lights for an all-bluegrass concert on July 4 at Oak Leaf Park in northern Virginia, including Bill Monroe and his Blue Grass Boys; the Stanley Brothers and the Clinch Mountain Boys; the Country Gentlemen; Jim and Jesse McReynolds; Mac Wiseman, a veteran of both Monroe's and Flatt and Scruggs' bands; and Clifton himself, a tobacco heir who had become the first city-boy bluegrass recording artist. The event, which drew more than two thousand people and featured reunions between Monroe and several former Blue Grass Boys, was a success, despite the refusal of two major bands—Flatt and Scruggs and the Foggy Mountain Boys, and Reno and Smiley and the Tennessee Cutups—to participate.

Ironically, it was Reno and Smiley's then-manager, Carlton Haney, who took the concept to the next level and organized the first full-fledged bluegrass festival. He had disagreed with Clifton's idea and kept Reno and Smiley from playing Clifton's concert but

The faithful gather for a bluegrass festival.

had attended and noted its success. When the Newport Folk Festival started drawing tens of thousands as the folk revival boomed in the early 1960s, Haney decided to organize something similar for bluegrass.

The event, held on Labor Day weekend in 1965, near Roanoke, Virginia, featured concerts, informal workshops, and a Sunday morning gospel sing. But the centerpiece of the festival, which would become an annual ritual within the ritual, was "The Story of Bluegrass," which Haney pulled together with the Newport Festival's Ralph Rinzler.

Rinzler had briefly served as Monroe's manager in 1963 and was deeply committed to helping Monroe win the recognition he deserved for his central role in the founding of bluegrass. On Sunday afternoon, a parade of former Blue Grass Boys, including Don Reno and Jimmy Martin, joined Monroe onstage in the order they had played with him, recreating various incarnations of the band. Haney, using information compiled by Rinzler, narrated the development of bluegrass as the invention of Monroe and his band, with each musician adding his own contribution to the mix. Flatt and Scruggs were not there (they were still not on speaking terms with Monroe), and Haney mentioned their part in the creation of bluegrass only briefly. But the Stanley Brothers performed; Carter Stanley sang a duet with Monroe and something momentous happened. After years of resenting the Stanleys as copycat competitors, Monroe praised them as the first group to follow in his footsteps. Rinzler had helped Monroe transform his bitterness toward those who had emulated his music into the magnanimous benevolence of a patriarch toward his children.

That first festival drew some one thousand people, from as far away as California. There were some culture clashes as well as inadequate water and toilet facilities, but there was enough enthusiasm and goodwill—and money—to justify a second annual gathering the next year and numerous emulators in later years. By April 1969, *Bluegrass Unlimited* magazine listed five bluegrass festivals in the upcoming season; two years later, Haney's new magazine, *Muleskinner News*, listed seventy-one events, including fiddlers' conventions and folk festivals as well as strictly bluegrass get-togethers. That year, Monroe started his own festival—which continues to this day—at Bean Blossom in southern Indiana, featuring a reconciliation between himself and Lester Flatt, as well as bands from New Zealand and Japan. Today, with more than five hundred bluegrass festivals across the country and some fifty more around the world, the festival circuit has fundamentally changed the economics of bluegrass. It has created opportunities for more musicians to turn professional and for established bands to make a decent living.

There have been growing pains over the years. The explosion of the counterculture in the late 1960s and the popularity of large outdoor music festivals, like Woodstock in 1969, drew larger crowds to bluegrass festivals in the 1970s. Many in the new audience were drawn more to generic outdoor musical happenings than specifically to bluegrass. The influx of young counterculture types (and the occasional motorcycle gang) added to tensions that are built into gatherings of the bluegrass clan, given bluegrass' appeal to both rural working-class people and middle-class urban and suburban people. For a while, conflicts over hair length and the Vietnam War were close to the surface; fistfights were common and shootings not unheard of. Now, although conflicts remain, they are seldom violent and are more likely to be about what constitutes "real" bluegrass than politics. And the lines are blurrier, with plenty of urban traditionalists and rural innovators.

The band recorded for Mercury from 1948 to 1950, cutting classics like "Roll in My Sweet Baby's Arms" and "Foggy Mountain Breakdown," which Warren Beatty used as the theme for his 1967 film, *Bonnie and Clyde.*

Scruggs kept innovating on the banjo. In 1951 he started retuning his strings in midsong to change keys and achieve a new sound. Probably to distinguish themselves from the Blue Grass Boys, Flatt and Scruggs never gave the mandolin much prominence; Curly Seckler sang superb tenor harmony, but, he recalls, he just "held the mandolin," which was virtually inaudible. The Dobro, played by Buck "Uncle Josh" Graves, who joined the Foggy Mountain Boys in 1955, was anything but inaudible. The first bluegrass player of the Dobro—a guitar with a metallic resonator embedded in its body and tuned to an open chord—Graves developed a highly syncopated style that emulated Scruggs' banjo picking.

Monroe resented the departure of his right-hand man and his star banjo player, but he resented the competition more. For years he prevailed on WSM to keep Flatt and Scruggs' band from a regular spot on the Grand Ole Opry. But in 1955, over Monroe's objections, the Foggy Mountain Boys won a coveted spot on the Opry cast.

It's Bluegrass

During the previous ten years, bluegrass had become an established genre within country music. Monroe wasn't flattered by the imitation, but the new sound had such an impact that numerous country musicians had picked up their mandolins and banjos, hiked up their pitch and speed, and begun making music in the style of the Blue Grass Boys.

The Stanley Brothers, Carter (left) and Ralph, sang songs that ached with loneliness and nostalgia for the old home place.

The Stanley Brothers, Carter (1925–1966) and Ralph (b. 1927), idolized Monroe. They would listen to the Grand Ole Opry on Saturday night and work up the Blue Grass Boys' new numbers with their band, the Clinch Mountain Boys, for their radio appearances the following week on WCYB. In 1947, Columbia released their version of "Molly and Tenbrooks," a horse-race song of black origin, arranged almost exactly as the Blue Grass Boys performed it. Ralph played three-finger banjo, and mandolinist Pee Wee Lambert sang a high Monroe-like lead. The recording prompted Monroe to move to Decca Records rather than stay on the same label as his imitators. The same year, former Opry performers the Bailey Brothers and the Happy Valley Boys, led by mandolinist Charlie Bailey and guitarist Danny Bailey, recorded "Rattlesnake Daddy Blues," which sounded quite similar to "Muleskinner Blues." Their instrumental "Happy Valley Special" showcased each band member just as "Blue Grass Special" did for the Blue Grass Boys.

The Stanleys went on to carve out a niche as the most old-fashioned of the first generation of bands playing the music that fans and deejays began calling "bluegrass" sometime around 1950. Carter wrote many of the group's songs

The Bailey Brothers, Charlie (left) and Danny, were one of several country groups that emulated Monroe's sound (not yet called bluegrass).

himself, penning religious and secular numbers that ached with loneliness. Ralph's high nasal harmony stood out, becoming almost a lead voice.

Don Reno replaced Scruggs in the Blue Grass Boys when he came home from the army but left the band in 1949 to form the Tennessee Cutups with singer-guitarist Red Smiley (1925–1972). Reno was a musical innovator

on the level of Scruggs and Monroe: he added jazzy riffs borrowed from the electric and steel guitars to his banjo playing. A prolific songwriter, Reno also composed banjo instrumentals in the fifties with new picking patterns and chord structures, beating a path that banjo experimenters like Bill Keith (b. 1939) and later Tony Trischka and Béla Fleck (b. circa 1953) would follow in decades to come. Reno was also among the first to play lead guitar with a flat-pick, influencing flat-pick guitar hero Doc Watson (b. 1923), who would in turn influence bluegrass guitar great Clarence White (1944–1973).

Reno recorded the first version of what is probably the best-known banjo tune ever, "Dueling Banjos," featured in the 1972 film *Deliverance*. "Dueling Banjos" was a rearrangement of "Feuding Banjos," which Reno recorded in 1955 with the tune's composer, his former boss, bandleader Arthur Smith (b. 1921). Unlike the movie version, which was a duel between banjo and guitar, the Smith-Reno version featured two banjos, with Reno on five-string and Smith on four-string. Smith would later win a lawsuit against Warner Bros. that established his authorship of the tune.

Several other former Blue Grass Boys went on to front their own successful bands in the early 1950s that are still active in some form today. Kentucky natives the Osborne Brothers, Bobby (b. 1931) and Sonny (b. 1937), who had played banjo with Bill Monroe in 1952, teamed up in 1954 with singer and guitarist Jimmy Martin, who was born in 1927 on a farm near Sneedville, Tennessee. Martin had played with the Blue Grass Boys on and off from 1950

Partisans of banjo innovator Don Reno (left, with partner Red Smiley) give him as much credit as Scruggs in creating the bluegrass banjo sound.

Singer-guitarist Jimmy Martin (left), who played with Monroe before starting his own Sunny Mountain Boys band, is passionate and opinionated about the music.

to 1954, succeeding Lester Flatt. His high, passionate vocals were a match for Monroe's, and his talent for rhythm guitar equaled or surpassed Flatt's. Monroe first recorded "Uncle Pen," his powerful tribute to his uncle, with Martin.

The Osborne Brothers recorded several songs with Martin before splitting up. The opinionated and outspoken Martin continued to uphold Monroe's banner of bluegrass tradition, while the Osbornes went on to pursue a more commercial path closer to mainstream country—for example, using drums on their recordings, starting in 1957. They created a new singing style that showcased Bobby's almost unearthly high voice. Instead of arranging the tenor harmony above the other voices, they put Sonny's high melody line on top, with baritone and tenor below it. They showcased this "high lead" style in "Ruby," which was a big hit for them in 1956, and they eventually won a regular slot on the Grand Ole Opry in 1964, which they still hold today.

Mac Wiseman has also successfully walked the often blurred line between bluegrass and (the rest of) country, combining hard-driving bluegrass instrumentation and a respect for tradition with openness to songs from pop and Nashville writers. Leaning more on his warm solo vocals than on ensemble harmonies, Wiseman has won considerable commercial success.

Another group that got their start in this period actually included no Blue Grass Boys alumni. When mandolinist Jesse McReynolds (b. 1929) heard Scruggs' banjo, he wanted to create a similar sound on his own instrument, and he developed a syncopated, note-laden style dubbed cross-picking. He formed a band with his brother, Jim (b. 1927), continuing in the brother duet tradition, with tight, high harmonies, and added Snuffy Jenkins' nephew Hoke on banjo in 1952.

Guitarists strive to emulate the "cross-picking" mandolin style of Jesse McReynolds (left, shown here with his brother, Jim), which was itself an attempt to translate Scruggs' banjo to the mandolin.

Between Hard Rock and Folk Plays

Country music was moving away from the string band sound and toward solo singing stars when the Blue Grass Boys took the Grand Ole Opry by storm. Hollywood had made movies featuring country figures such as Roy Acuff and Ernest Tubb (1914–1984), but Monroe did not dominate the spotlight in his band the way Acuff and Tubb did, and a band can't star in a movie. A 1942–1944 musicians' union strike had the unintended effect of accelerating the trend toward featured singers with bands in the background by preventing most bands from recording but allowing the release of records by singers (who weren't part of the strike because they weren't allowed in the union). That taught the captains of the country music industry that had grown up around the Opry in Nashville that they could make records more profitably with singers backed by studio musicians than with bands.

So bluegrass was already bucking country music trends in the mid-1950s, when black rhythm and blues exploded onto the pop charts as rock and

Opposite: Blind guitarist Doc Watson (left) rapidly picks out melodies note for note. He was influenced by Don Reno and, in turn, influenced countless bluegrass guitar players. Below: Elvis threw bluegrassers—and the rest of the country music world—for a loop.

roll. The success of country boy Elvis Presley put further pressure on bluegrass and other country musicians to update their sound. Then, in the late 1950s, folk music became the rage, as the Kingston Trio's "Tom Dooley" hit number one on the pop charts, creating a demand for "pure" acoustic music. Bluegrass bands responded differently to these contradictory pressures.

Surprisingly, given their generally traditional bent, the Stanley Brothers recorded the rock-flavored song "So Blue" and covered the R&B number "Finger Popping Time." The Osborne Brothers and Jim and Jesse added to their music elements of the "Nashville Sound," which was the response of producers like Chet Atkins (b. 1924), himself an excellent guitar picker, to rock and roll. Atkins tried to engineer a middle-of-the-road sound that, by eliminating the really rural-

sounding instruments—particularly fiddle and banjo—and adding vocal cho-
ruses, electric guitars, and drums, created music that was still country but could
win younger audiences as well. The Osbornes, for example, added an electric-
bass player to their band in 1967 and included pedal steel when they recorded
their biggest hit to date, "Rocky Top," one of a series of successes penned for the
Osbornes by the husband-and-wife duo Felice (b. 1925) and Boudleaux Bryant
(1920–1987).

Monroe by and large resisted the modernizing trend, although he did
record a sped-up version of "Blue Moon of Kentucky" after Presley hit with his
rockabilly version. But he also remained obscure, at first, to folk music devotees.

Folk fans had, however, discovered Earl Scruggs, who brought the
house down at the first Newport Folk Festival in 1959 (where the Stanley
Brothers also appeared). Folk enthusiasts' premium on purity made some uneasy
at first with bluegrass, which, with its up-tempo songs and instrumental virtuos-
ity, smacked to some of commercialism. But folklorist Alan Lomax (b. 1915) put
his imprimatur on the music in the October 1959 issue of *Esquire* magazine,
calling bluegrass "folk music with overdrive" and lionizing Flatt and Scruggs.
Reviewing the Newport Festival, the *New York Times'* Robert Shelton wrote

*The 1950s–1960s boom in the popularity of folk singers like the Kingston Trio helped
win a new, urban audience for bluegrass.*

As the folk boom moved into folk-rock, Scruggs turned on to the new sound and joined his sons, Gary (left) and Randy (right), jamming on their electric instruments.

that Scruggs bore "about the same relationship to the banjo that Paganini does to the violin." Scruggs met rising folk star Joan Baez (b. 1941) backstage at Newport, a connection his wife and manager, Louise, would exploit, hooking the band up with Baez's Boston-based booking agent Manny Greenhill, whose clients also included folksinger Pete Seeger (b. 1919).

Louise, who had a keen business sense, helped the Foggy Mountain Boys capitalize on the folk boom by writing album liner notes, promotional materials, and songbook copy for the band that emphasized their folk roots. By 1963, they had played at colleges and folk clubs across the country, as well as at Carnegie Hall, and were making annual television appearances on CBS' *The Beverly Hillbillies*, whose theme Flatt and Scruggs wrote.

When the folk music magazine *Sing Out!* called Scruggs "the undisputed master of bluegrass music" in 1962, Ralph Rinzler (1934–1994), a key figure in the folk revival, decided to let the folk world know about Bill Monroe. Having grown up listening to Library of Congress field recordings of blues and hillbilly musicians, he had been introduced to bluegrass at Swarthmore College. Rinzler learned to play mandolin and was one of many young northerners

who made trips south to hear bluegrass and old-time musicians, discover new talent, and enter music contests. He joined one of the first "citybilly" bluegrass bands, the New York City–based Greenbriar Boys, which also included John Herald (b. 1939) on guitar and Bob Yellin on banjo. He first heard Monroe

While Scruggs (above, left) plugged in, Monroe (above) remained a rock-ribbed traditionalist.

at a country music park in 1954 and had been deeply impressed. Monroe was suspicious when Rinzler asked for an interview, but eventually granted the request, and Rinzler's article, "Bill Monroe, the Daddy of Bluegrass," appeared in *Sing Out!* in January 1963. Rinzler arranged for a couple of concerts for folk audiences in Chicago and New York early that year, and shortly afterward moved to Nashville to become Monroe's manager.

He arrived not a moment too soon, as Monroe's career was at a low ebb. Monroe didn't have enough regular, well-paying bookings to keep his musicians on salary, making it difficult to keep a top-notch band together, and he was laboring under a weight of resentment and envy of former protégés who had made it big (or at least bigger than he had). The folk bookings that Rinzler arranged brought Monroe a larger audience, reviving his finances, and attracted a flock of young citybilly musicians to play with him, reviving his sound. Rinzler's promotion of Monroe as the father of the genre helped Monroe see other bluegrass musicians as family rather than rivals. He began talking more to his audiences and to interviewers about his life and music.

Bostonian Bill Keith was one of the first city-boy musicians to join Monroe, in 1963. Having studied the four-string banjo played with a pick, he had developed a way to play fiddle tunes note-for-note on the five-string banjo, going beyond standard Scruggs style. Inspired by the bluegrass music on tap at Boston's Hillbilly Ranch tavern in the 1950s and 1960s, he helped form the Charles River Boys, one of the first northern bluegrass bands. Keith's "chromatic" style sent pickers rushing to their instruments to figure out his tunes, much the same way Scruggs' playing had influenced musicians twenty years before. Monroe praised Keith's banjo style to the skies, but Keith's stint with the Blue Grass Boys was a short one. He left after less than a year, partly because he was tired of the band's grueling tour schedule and partly because Monroe had agreed to perform on ABC's *Hootenanny* television program, which had black-listed Pete Seeger, Keith's earlier role model, for his left-wing politics. But with his stature now established, Monroe was able to draw on a pool of talented young musicians eager to play with the founder of bluegrass.

The Country Gentlemen and
Progressive Bluegrass

Meanwhile, in the Washington, D.C., area, a new kind of bluegrass band had come on the scene in 1957. The Country Gentlemen, comprising Texas-born Charlie Waller (b. 1935) on mandolin, D.C.–area native John Duffey (b. 1934) on guitar, and, by 1959, Virginia-born banjoist Eddie Adcock (b. 1938), mixed together old hillbilly numbers learned from records and folk revival tunes like "Tom Dooley" with Adcock's banjo, which had been influenced by Chet Atkins' guitar work. The Gentlemen added to this mix casual, ad-libbed humor, which was a real departure from bluegrass up to that point: older bands used more scripted, vaudeville-style comedy if they went for laughs at all, and Monroe was dead serious, even earnest, onstage, despite the fact that his 1940s tent shows had included comedy acts. The Gents, however, cracked up audiences with their antics, which even extended to doing impressions of Monroe as well as a spoof of the Kingston Trio.

The Country Gentlemen recorded "Tom Dooley" in 1959 as a single for Starday, then the biggest label specializing in bluegrass, but Duffey couldn't persuade Starday's Don Pierce to put out a Country Gentlemen album. Duffey succeeded in selling it to Moses Asch at the folk and ethnic music label Folkways. *Country Songs Old and New* was just that, including old ballads like "Jesse James" and "Ellen Smith" as well as a new song in ballad form, Marijohn Wilkin and Danny Dill's "Long Black Veil," which had been a country hit for Lefty Frizzell (1928–1975). The Gents also did originals, such as Duffey's "Bringing Mary Home," which was based on the popular urban folktale of the vanishing hitchhiker and hit the country charts briefly in 1965.

The Country Gentlemen became the anchor of a strong bluegrass scene in the Washington area, which, like the Great Lakes industrial belt, had drawn a substantial migration of people from the Appalachian Mountains. The mid-1950s

The Washington-area band the Country Gentlemen (shown here in the 1970s) were among the first to apply bluegrass instrumentation to rock songs in the late 1950s.

*The traditionally oriented Stonemans, led by patriarch Ernest "Pop" Stoneman (seated),
were another anchor of a burgeoning D.C. bluegrass scene.*

D.C. scene also included traditional bands like the Stoneman Family, made up
of the children of legendary hillbilly recording star Ernest "Pop" Stoneman
(1893–1968). The band's banjoist, Veronica Stoneman Cox, was featured on
the first long-playing record of bluegrass music, Folkways' *American Banjo
Music Scruggs Style*, and was later a regular on the *Hee Haw* television program. The region would become known, however, for "progressive" (as opposed
to traditional) bluegrass.

For progressive bluegrass musicians, what makes a tune bluegrass is a
set of instruments and a musical method that can be applied to almost any song.
For example, New Shades of Grass, one band Duffey worked with after leaving
the Gentlemen in 1969, drew heavily from contemporary rock, recording songs
by Creedence Clearwater Revival and the South African rocker Manfred Mann
(b. 1940). New Shades of Grass, which included banjoist Bill Emerson (b.
1938), Dobro virtuoso Mike Auldridge, and guitarist Cliff Waldron (b. 1941),
recorded Mann's "Fox on the Run" in 1969, and it is now a bluegrass chest-
nut. Adcock left the Gentlemen in 1971 to found The II Generation. Multi-in-
strumentalist Doyle Lawson played with the Country Gentlemen in the early

Women in Bluegrass

What do women cite most often as the biggest obstacle to success in bluegrass? It's not the traditional songs that have about three slots for women: blue-eyed darlin', jezebel, and aged mother; it's not the men who turn jam sessions into competitions or "borrow" instruments and then don't return them; it's not the unequally shared domestic responsibilities that leave no time to practice, let alone tour; it's not even conservative attitudes about women's roles in the bluegrass heartland of the rural South. Although women have complained about all of these, it often comes down to keys.

The average woman's voice is pitched in an unsuitable range to sing bluegrass songs in the keys in which they are conventionally sung—the keys in which male musicians learn their instrumental breaks and vocal harmonies. When a woman comes to a jam session and wants to kick off a song in D, she's likely to get the hairy eyeball from the male banjo picker who's worked out his licks in G and the tenor singer who can't find his harmony line. (Ironically, bluegrass patriarch Bill Monroe is an inveterate key-changer, starting songs wherever his voice feels right on a given day.)

It's more than just technical, of course. High-pitched singing is central to the bluegrass sound, and traditionally it's the struggle to reach the high notes that puts the "lonesome" in the high lonesome sound. ("If it don't hurt it ain't bluegrass" is a common belief.) Since women generally don't have to work as hard as men to reach the high notes, some hard-core traditionalists believe women can't sing bluegrass. So although women have traditionally been able to break into other musical genres as singers, they've had an extra challenge in becoming bluegrass artists.

Nonetheless, women have been contributing to bluegrass since before it started. Maybelle Carter and her cousin, Sara Carter, sang lead and played all the instruments in the Carter Family, a group that deeply influenced bluegrass. The Coon Creek Girls were an exciting Kentucky string band in the thirties and forties that in some ways anticipated the bluegrass sound. Fiddler Howdy Forrester's wife, Sally Forrester, played the accordion—one of the instruments Bill Monroe's mother used to play—in a pre-bluegrass version of Monroe's band. Donna Stoneman played mandolin and her sister Veronica Stoneman Cox played the banjo with the Stoneman Family. (Conservative southern audiences were willing to put aside the old-world notion that a stageful of men is no place for a respectable woman—as long as the woman was in the men's family.) Behind the scenes, a canny Louise Scruggs masterminded the career of her husband, Earl.

Country singers Rose Maddox and Dian James each recorded albums with bluegrass backing in 1962. But it wasn't until the explosion of the women's movement in the late sixties and early seventies that significant numbers of women began making bluegrass music themselves, outside their families. At first, the surge occurred primarily in the San Francisco Bay area and other places removed

from restrictive rural attitudes. California-born fiddler/singer/songwriter Laurie Lewis once told an International Bluegrass Music Association audience that she hadn't realized she wasn't supposed to play bluegrass—so she just went ahead.

Today, there is a newsletter for women in bluegrass, edited by banjoist Murphy Henry, who also teaches banjo, produces bluegrass instruction videos, and plays in a band with her husband and children. There are now dozens of women fronting mixed bands, from current sensation Alison Krauss to Lewis to traditionalist leading light Lynn Morris to songwriter/guitarists Claire Lynch and Kathy Chiavola. They have joined a club of which Grand Ole Opry veteran Wilma Lee Cooper (b. 1921) was long the only member. There are dozens more all-female bands: the All Girl Boys, Local Tomatoes, Petticoat Junction, and Bluegrass Liberation, to name a few.

All this progress notwithstanding, an International Bluegrass Music Association convention not too long ago featured an ad hoc band of hot young players, billed as the future of bluegrass—and they were all male. When Henry complained, organizers said they hadn't been able to find any female players on short notice. But that won't happen again: Henry started a database of women bluegrassers that now has about a thousand names.

Opposite: Maybelle Carter is a foremother of bluegrass women. Top: Turned down by several top bands, Lynn Morris started her own group. Bottom: Alison Krauss sings like an angel and fiddles like the devil.

Ricky Skaggs went from traditional bluegrass to country stardom via the Country Gentlemen and The New South.

1970s and since 1979 has fronted Quicksilver, known even more for their shining a cappella harmonies on gospel songs than for their undeniably high-caliber instrumental work.

Duffey and Auldridge started playing with some friends they met at a picking party—banjoist Ben Eldridge, guitarist John Starling, and bass player Tom Gray. Word got around that the five were forming a band, and the Gents' Waller asked Auldridge, "I keep hearing this rumor that you guys have this band. What do you call yourselves—The Seldom Seen?" The name stuck, slightly altered to the Seldom Scene, and they are still one of the most popular bands in bluegrass, despite the fact that they all maintain day jobs and play part-time.

Mainstream country star Ricky Skaggs (b. 1954) is another alumnus of the Country Gentlemen, and his path from bluegrass to country stardom is an interesting one. As a child, he played with Monroe and with Flatt and Scruggs. He then teamed up as a teenager with fellow Kentuckian Keith Whitley (1955–1989) and performed close imitations of Stanley Brothers songs. When Ralph Stanley met them at a small club in Louisa, Kentucky, a few years after Carter Stanley had died in 1966 of a liver ailment, he was amazed and touched by their uncannily close emulations of the Stanley Brothers sound. The pair did some recording and touring with Stanley and the Clinch Mountain Boys for a couple of years before Skaggs left to play with the Country Gentlemen. His next hitch was with another important band, J.D. Crowe and The New South, before working with Emmylou Harris in the late 1970s and going solo, hitting the country charts in 1981 with, among other songs, the Flatt and Scruggs number "Don't Get Above Your Raisin'."

Another progressive bluegrasser who has made a bid for crossover into mainstream country is mandolinist/singer/songwriter Tim O'Brien. From the late 1970s through the 1980s, O'Brien was a mainstay of the smoking Denver-based band Hot Rize, named for the self-rising ingredient in Martha White Flour, a company that had sponsored Flatt and Scruggs. Along with guitarist Charles Sawtelle and demon banjoist Pete Wernick, who wrote an influential banjo instruction book, O'Brien helped Hot Rize develop a high energy, contemporary sound. Hot Rize also played honky-tonk country music, creating an alter-ego band, Red Knuckles and the Trailblazers, to do so. Wearing Stetsons and shades, the Trailblazers played with genuine enthusiasm but also with a strong dose of 1980s irony. After country star Kathy Mattea recorded several of his songs, O'Brien split from Hot Rize in 1989 and went solo, crafting a fluid mix of country, jazz, bluegrass, western swing, pop, and even traditional Irish music.

Most progressive bands cultivated a sophisticated, uptown sound and repertoire, partially to distinguish themselves from bluegrass' hayseed image, promoted by *The Beverly Hillbillies* and other television programs; J.D. Crowe and The New South took a more mixed approach. They were led by Lexington, Kentucky, native and banjoist J.D. Crowe (b. 1937), who had two major musical passions: the banjo and the blues. He was equally fascinated as a youth by Earl Scruggs and Fats Domino (b. 1928), and incorporated blues guitar elements into his banjo picking. So, like the Gents, The New South did plenty of contemporary material—recording Fats Domino and Dave Bartholemew's "I'm Walkin," for example. But they also brought new life to classics like Lester Flatt's "Why Don't You Tell Me So?" rendering them with respect and instrumental fire.

In addition to Skaggs and Crowe, The New South included Jerry Douglas (b. 1956)—whose virtuoso Dobro style is distinct from the Josh Graves/Mike Auldridge school—and guitarist/lead singer Tony Rice (b. 1951). Rice's lead vocals were unusual for bluegrass—somewhat mellower

The Dillards, led by banjoist Doug Dillard, incorporated comic antics as well as instrumental wizardry into their performances.

and lower-pitched than the average lead singer—and his guitar playing was extraordinary, featuring shining, jazzy, bluesy, yet sensitive flat-pick leads that were never merely flashy.

Meanwhile, in California

Tony Rice, a Californian with Appalachian roots, patterned his picking on that of Clarence White, who was born in Maine of French-Canadian extraction and whose father moved the family to California when Clarence was ten years old. Clarence and his older brother, mandolinist Roland, were the core of the Kentucky Colonels, a short-lived but influential Los Angeles–based band in the early 1960s. Clarence was agog when he heard guitarist Doc Watson at L.A.'s premier folk club, the Ash Grove. Watson, playing solo, picked fiddle tunes note-for-note with ease and fluidity while keeping rock-solid rhythm. Bluegrass lead guitarists like Don Reno usually needed rhythm backup, but Watson did both. White got to work figuring out how it was done and was the first guitarist to combine lead and rhythm work in a bluegrass band. White would eventually join the folk-rock band The Byrds, playing with them from 1968 to 1973. He was in the process of reuniting the Kentucky Colonels when he was killed by a drunken driver in 1973. Roland White later played with Lester Flatt and is currently a member of the highly regarded Nashville Bluegrass Band.

Another pair of brothers was the nucleus of important California bluegrass band The Dillards. Banjo wizard Doug Dillard (b. 1937) and his brother Rodney (b. 1942), a singer and guitarist, along with mandolinist Dean Webb (b. 1937) and bassist Mitchell Jayne (b. 1930), just showed up at the Ash Grove one night in 1962 and started playing in the lobby. The Dillard brothers' father was an old-time fiddler; they had grown up in the Ozarks and just arrived from Missouri, but they were not rubes. Their dazzling sound drew the audience—and eventually the evening's performers, the Greenbriar Boys—into the lobby to hear them. In short order, the Greenbriars' Ralph Rinzler helped them get a contract with Elektra, a major label that was producing a fair amount of folk music at the time. They played to folk revival audiences around the country, including the one at the Newport Festival, and were the first bluegrass band to record a song by Bob Dylan (b. 1941), "Walking Down the Line," in 1964. (The Country Gentlemen would later also record it.)

Fiddler Byron Berline (b. 1944) met the Dillards backstage after their November 1962 gig at the University of Oklahoma, where he was a student. Doug Dillard and Berline, whose father was also a fiddler, got to swapping tunes, and Dillard was impressed by Berline's Texas contest-style fiddling. Berline had won the first fiddle contest he entered at age ten, beating his father at playing the jazzy, highly ornamented, and rhythmically complex style, with numerous variations on the tune. He recorded the album *Pickin' and Fiddlin'* with The Dillards on his summer break in 1964. Bill

Fiddler Byron Berline (top, right) gave bluegrass another infusion of Texas swing.

Folk-rockers the Flying Burrito Brothers added a bluegrass segment, including Byron Berline, to their shows in 1971.

Monroe offered him a job after hearing him at Newport the following year, but Berline wanted to finish college first; just a few months after joining the Blue Grass Boys in 1967, he was drafted. When he was discharged, Monroe's favorite fiddler, Kenny Baker, was back with the band, and Berline headed to L.A. where he was soon in great demand for session work.

In 1971, the folk-rock band the Flying Burrito Brothers, which included former Byrd Chris Hillman, started adding a bluegrass segment to the middle of their performances, and Berline signed on to play in that slot. When the Burrito Brothers broke up the following year, Berline and the other bluegrassers, bass player Roger Bush and guitarist Kenny Wertz, formed Country Gazette, which banjoist Alan Munde, a University of Oklahoma classmate of Berline's, joined soon after. In 1995, Berline created bluegrass history, bringing together Bill Monroe and Earl Scruggs for the first time in a studio since they split up; they recorded "Sally Goodin," a Texas contest-style showstopper that became a bluegrass standard after Berline introduced it to Monroe's repertoire in 1967.

Newgrass

Among the participants in a huge jam session centered around Byron Berline at a 1968 Texas fiddle contest was teenage mandolinist Sam Bush (b. 1952), who was on leave from the army. Within six months, Bush and two other participants in that session, Munde and guitarist Wayne Stewart, recorded *Poor Richard's Almanac*, an album heavily influenced by Berline's swinging sound. Three years later, Bush founded New Grass Revival, which took bluegrass instrumentation into a whole different musical world. They were the first counterculture bluegrass band. They sported long hair (which prompted Monroe to bar them from his Bean Blossom bluegrass festival in 1972 unless they got haircuts), and their electric-bass player, John Cowan, cited the Beatles as his major musical influence. They incorporated long, free-form improvised instrumentals, à la modern jazz, Indian ragas, and Bay Area rock. Their sound was more lush and orchestral than the usual bluegrass band. Their plugged-in instruments freed them from standing still in front of microphones onstage and allowed them to move with the music like rock and rollers, and also like the black plantation banjo players who had helped start it all two centuries ago.

A later incarnation of the group would include jazz-oriented banjo genius Béla Fleck, and "newgrass" became the name of a new school (barely) within bluegrass. Part of the impetus for newgrass came from Earl Scruggs. Like many in the folk revival, he and his sons, Randy, Steve, and Gary, were increasingly interested in electric instruments, and folk fans had become increasingly tolerant of electricity over the past several years, despite the controversy that erupted when Bob Dylan plugged in at the 1965 Newport Festival.

In the mid- to late 1960s, Scruggs' electric inclinations got a boost from record producers who wanted to cash in on the counterculture, and Flatt and

New Grass Revival just before they broke up in 1989 featured (left to right) fiddler/ mandolinist Sam Bush, guitarist Pat Flynn, bassist John Cowan, and banjo wizard Béla Fleck.

Vassar Clements came back from a bout with alcoholism to help invigorate the jazzy "newgrass" subgenre, playing with Jerry Garcia, among others.

Scruggs recorded covers of songs by Donovan, The Lovin' Spoonful, The Monkees, and Dylan. But Flatt hated the new material and the drug-taking hippies he associated with it. The pair was held together temporarily by the success of their soundtrack for *Bonnie and Clyde* in 1967 but finally split up in 1969. Flatt founded a new band called The Nashville Grass, reconciled with Monroe, and kept playing traditional bluegrass until he died in 1979. Scruggs and his plugged-in sons formed the Earl Scruggs Revue, and Scruggs also worked on a number of recording projects. The biggest of these was the 1972 triple album *Will the Circle Be Unbroken*, which brought together country rock group The Nitty Gritty Dirt Band with country legends Maybelle Carter, Roy Acuff, and Merle Travis; Doc Watson; and bluegrass musicians Jimmy Martin and Vassar Clements (b. 1928).

Fiddler Vassar Clements, who played with Monroe in 1949 and Jim and Jesse from 1958 to 1961, moved into newgrass in 1975. That year he recorded the album *Old and In the Way* with fiddler/guitarist/singer/songwriter Peter Rowan, one of Monroe's citybillies in the mid 1960s; mandolinist David Grisman; and the Grateful Dead's Jerry Garcia (1942–1995). In the San Francisco Bay area, Grisman would later lead the David Grisman Quintet, which included Tony Rice, out of bluegrass entirely in the late 1970s and into what he called "dawg music" or "jazz grass" and what Rice called "space grass"—essentially a combination of bluegrass instrumentation with complex jazz chord structures.

Bluegrass by the Bay

The San Francisco Bay area was also home to a band that started as a one-gig lark and helped launch the careers of some of bluegrass' most important recent masters, including several of the first women to achieve bluegrass prominence.

The Good Ol' Persons were fronted by Kathy Kallick (center), whose use of minor chords, ambivalence, and irony was unusual for bluegrass.

One day in 1975, singer/guitarist Kathy Kallick (b. 1952) persuaded fiddler/singer Laurie Lewis (b. 1950) to pull together a group of women to go into Paul's Saloon, the center of San Francisco's bluegrass scene, and play a set. Lewis, winner of dozens of fiddle contests, corralled bassist Sue Shelasky, who was in the band Phantoms of the Opry with Lewis, and a couple of others, and the Good Ol' Persons took Paul's by storm. The band became known for fast-paced but never sloppy renditions of traditional bluegrass with classic country and a little swing thrown in. Sally Van Meter (b. 1956), a world-class Dobro player on the level of Auldridge and Douglas, contributed a unique sound that harked back to the Dobro's parent, the bottleneck blues guitar. Mandolinist John Reischman (b. 1955) ("The band was infiltrated early on by men," Kallick once told *Bluegrass Unlimited*) picked cleanly and got more brightness from the instrument than many could. And Kallick was in the top ranks of bluegrass singer/songwriters, penning numbers that ached with ambivalence and wistfulness and singing them in a throaty, sultry soprano.

Lewis left the Persons; spent some time in Peter Rowan's band, the Free Mexican Air Force; learned to make fiddles and took over an instrument shop in Berkeley; taught fiddle, bass, and singing; and played in pickup bands at Paul's. The Grant Street String Band, named for her Berkeley address, emerged

Fiddler Laurie Lewis (left), one of the original Good Ol' Persons, didn't know women weren't supposed to play bluegrass.

from those casual groupings. At the instigation of Washington, D.C. area banjo picker Cathy Fink, Lewis and Van Meter joined Fink, mandolin and guitar player Marcy Marxer, and bassist Molly Mason for a one-album, all-women "super-group," Blue Rose, in 1988. Meanwhile her band, whose name was now shortened to Grant Street, was winning over enthusiastic audiences across the country. Lewis' well-crafted original songs, smooth and sweet but never syrupy soprano (often twined in exquisite harmonies around the voice of mandolinist Tom Rozum), and her equally smooth fiddling anchor the band. In addition to Lewis' songs, Grant Street's eclectic repertoire includes Jimmie Rodgers yodels, songs from brother duets like the Everlys and the Louvins, and old traditional numbers. The band's former banjo player, newgrass-influenced Tony Furtado, was only the second person to win the National Banjo Championship, at the Walnut Valley Festival in Winfield, Kansas, twice.

Back to the Grass Roots

The first two-time National Banjo Champion was Lynn Morris, who won in 1974 and again in 1981. She now fronts one of the best of several bands promoting a revival of traditional bluegrass, but there was a period in the late

1980s when she had trouble getting work. Born in western Texas, she encountered bluegrass for the first time at Colorado College in the late 1960s. She then moved to Denver and cofounded City Limits, a bluegrass trio, which played together from 1972 to 1978. In 1982, banjoist Pete Wernick, of Hot Rize, hooked her up with Whetstone Run, a well-established band based in central Pennsylvania. On the way to join the group, she made a stopover to visit her sister in San Antonio. There she met bass player Marshall Wilborn (b. 1952) at a jam session; the pair became fast friends, and he was visiting her in Pennsylvania when Whetstone Run's bassist quit and they offered him the job.

Whetstone Run split up in 1986, and Wilborn was offered a job with the Washington-area band the Johnson Mountain Boys, who had helped start the new traditional trend in bluegrass. Wilborn and Morris, now a couple, moved to northern Virginia, and Morris tried in vain to win auditions for all-male traditional bands. When the Johnson Mountain Boys disbanded (temporarily, as it turns out), Morris, Wilborn, and former Johnson Mountain Boys banjoist Tom Adams solved the problem by forming the Lynn Morris Band, with Morris at that point on guitar and sharing lead singing duties with Wilborn.

As a woman, leading a traditional bluegrass band has posed numerous challenges for Morris, not least of which is repertoire. As much as she loves the old songs, she refuses to sing any that cast women as helpless victims or jezebels. Fortunately Wilborn is a talented songwriter, and by picking and choosing among old songs and songs by writers as diverse as Buck Owens (b. 1929) and Hazel Dickens (b. 1935), the band has won audience acclaim from coast to coast. Adams left the band in 1992 to join the reconstituted Johnson Mountain Boys, prompting Morris to move from the guitar back to the banjo, and she is now one of the few banjo players in bluegrass to mix in some of the older clawhammer playing with Scruggs picking.

When guitarist/singer Dudley Connell (b. 1956) pulled together the band that would become the Johnson Mountain Boys to play classic bluegrass in bars and bluegrass clubs around Washington in 1976, the initial response was far from overwhelming. They were playing old songs aching with loneliness and sentiment, and they refused to do requests for contemporary bluegrass hits—

because they didn't know them. Eventually they developed a devoted following; their old sound was actually fresh in the capital of progressive bluegrass. They put their instruments at the service of the songs, as opposed to showing off instrumental skill for its own sake, and they sang with conviction and emotional commitment.

The band's personnel has evolved over the years, with Connell's mournful, vibrato-laced tenor and crisp guitar playing and Eddie Stubbs' smoky, bluesy fiddle and bass vocals at the core. The band took the bluegrass festival circuit by storm, and recorded a series of classic albums that featured obscure gems learned from the records of bluegrass masters balanced with Connell's traditional-sounding originals and the occasional slower country song, delivered in Stubbs' smooth, deep voice, reminiscent of Ernest Tubb. Low pay and constant touring put a strain on the band as several members started families, and the group bid a tearful farewell in a 1988 concert in a northern Virginia schoolhouse. A couple of years later, however, at the urging of several friends, they regrouped and began playing a limited number of gigs a year, finding that they could play less and enjoy it more.

One of the friends who nudged the Johnson Mountain Boys out of their retirement was Ron Thomason, another leader of bluegrass's younger traditionalists. Thomason, a mandolinist who fronts the Ohio-based Dry Branch Fire Squad, is a serious preacher about the gospel of the old-time sound, but his message is usually side-splittingly funny. Born in Appalachian southern Ohio, he has a love for the music and culture of the mountains, and the band is often called a missing link between old-time mountain music and bluegrass. Thomason deflates stereotypes about country people by parodying and exaggerating them, and he jokes on stage about the music he loves. "The banjo does so have a purpose," he told a folk festival audience. "Without it all bluegrass songs wouldn't sound the same!"

Thomason played with Ralph Stanley in the 1970s, leaving to form the Fire Squad just as Keith Whitley and Ricky Skaggs joined Stanley's band. The members of the band have changed over the years, but all have one thing in common: day jobs. While the ideal for most musicians is to make music full-time, Thomason objects for philosophical reasons. He likes his music with rough edges,

Recently rediscovered traditionalist Del McCoury (center) has a voice that penetrates like a laser beam.

played for love, and believes playing full-time puts too much pressure on the music: pressure to play what's popular so you get more bookings, pressure to play too many gigs because you need the money.

The band can play their instruments just fine, but it's the passionate vocals from Thomason, longtime rhythm guitarist Mary Jo Leet, and recently joined guitarist and clawhammer banjo player Suzanne Thomas that really stand out. You can smell the sweat of the congregation and hear the amens when the Squad tears into the gospel number "Church by the Road." The group's reverence for tradition is idiosyncratic, though. A recent recording included "Carolyn at the Broken Wheel Inn," a honky-tonk number that features Dan Russell, who usually plays banjo, on electric pedal steel guitar. That ticked off purists, who wondered in print if the Squad would dare play the offending instrument onstage.

Del McCoury (b. 1930) has kept the traditional flag waving since 1963, when he played for a year with Bill Monroe, but has only recently reaped the success he deserved. He came to the Blue Grass Boys as a banjo player, but Monroe moved him to the guitar/lead singer slot to make room for Bill Keith. That was a significant choice, since McCoury, a western North Carolina native, has a high, piercing laser beam of a voice that raises the hairs on the back of one's neck. He left the Blue Grass Boys about the same time as Keith and worked with him in a band called the Shady Valley Boys. McCoury founded his own group, the Dixie Pals, in 1967, and they toiled in relative obscurity for well over

Bluegrass for the Masses

Thanks to a spate of movies, television programs, and commercials from the early 1960s through the mid-1970s, baby boomers now think they know what bluegrass is: it's that fast-paced banjo music played by dim-witted hillbillies that accompanies 1930s gangsters as they make love or make their getaway.

Perhaps the first use of bluegrass music in a soundtrack was in 1962 in filmmaker Joe Anderson's *Football as It Is Played Today*. This experimental short follows an Ohio State game, covering the whole event in five minutes—from rolling up the tarp covering the field through the game and the halftime show to the emptying of the stadium—through the use of time-lapse photography, which appears to speed up motion. A few months later, Anderson made *How Swived* for a CBS special. It depicted the frenetic life of a housewife by filming her in time lapse with a bluegrass soundtrack. A few months later, the Ford Motor Company started airing a commercial showing a station wagon zipping around town in time lapse—with a bluegrass soundtrack.

At about the same time, television producer Paul Henning heard Flatt and Scruggs play at the Los Angeles folk club the Ash Grove and decided that he had found the people to play the incidental music he needed for his new CBS sitcom, *The Beverly Hillbillies*. Flatt and Scruggs didn't like the idea much. They had worked hard to win the respect of sophisticated urban audiences and were not enthusiastic about reinforcing the typical hillbilly stereotype.

But Henning eventually won them over; they recorded the theme song, "The Ballad of Jed Clampett," and made annual cameos on the program from 1962 to 1968. The song hit both the bluegrass and country charts and in early 1963 became the first bluegrass song to top the country charts. (Incidentally, the rich bass voice on the soundtrack, so unlike

the high, lonesome singing typical in bluegrass, is not Flatt but Hollywood singer Jerry Scroggins.) Flatt and Scruggs would later record theme songs for two more CBS comedies, *Petticoat Junction* and *Green Acres*.

Also in 1962, Elektra's signing of the hot Los Angeles–based band The Dillards got the attention of the producers of CBS' *The Andy Griffith Show*. By the start of 1963, The Dillards were making regular appearances on the show, purveying their flashy musicianship and homespun Ozark Mountain humor as the fictional Darlin family.

Five years later, Warren Beatty used Flatt and Scruggs' classic instrumental "Foggy Mountain Breakdown" and some other bluegrass tunes in *Bonnie and Clyde*, which Beatty produced and starred in. The music was historically inaccurate—Bill Monroe was just starting to play professionally with his brother, Charlie, and bluegrass was a gleam off his mandolin pick in 1934 when gangsters Clyde Barrow and Bonnie Parker were killed. But it worked as accompaniment for the pair's holdups and for their climactic love scene just

before they are ambushed; the movie was a hit, and so was "Foggy Mountain Breakdown" for Flatt and Scruggs. They wore gangster suits and toted guns instead of instruments on the cover of the soundtrack album, which included songs about the gangster couple by Nashville songwriter Tom T. Hall. After the movie, bluegrass-soundtracked television commercials were ubiquitous for a couple of years.

Perhaps the most powerful bluegrass image in popular culture is from the 1972 film *Deliverance*, based on a 1970 James Dickey novel. The film tells the story of four Atlanta men whose canoe trip in the Ozarks turns into a nightmare confrontation with a group of mountain men. In the most famous scene, the Atlantans stop for gas, and one of them starts a musical conversation with a vacant-eyed, toothless youth by picking a few notes on his guitar. The youth responds with a few notes from the banjo held slack on his lap; the pair trade phrases, and the exchange quickly becomes a contest, which the mountain boy wins handily, picking Scruggs-style rings around the guitarist before retreating again into his own world. The musical confrontation presages the later, extremely violent clash in the woods while also showing the existence of points of commonality between the rural and urban worlds.

After the film came out, something of a rural-urban conflict ensued over rights to the tune that emerged from the two characters' contest. New York City banjoist Eric Weissberg dubbed it "Dueling Banjos" when he recorded it with guitarist Steve Mandell for the *Deliverance* soundtrack. The movie studio, Warner Brothers, copyrighted it in his name, and it hit the pop charts. Versions of the tune had been recorded several times before *Deliverance*, however: by The Dillards in 1963 as "Duelin' Banjo"; by Carl Story and The Brewster Brothers in 1957 as "Mocking Banjo"; and originally as a duel between country bandleader Arthur Smith's four-string banjo and Don Reno's five-string, which the pair recorded as "Feuding Banjo" in 1955. Smith sued Warner Bros. and eventually won royalties.

The film's damage cannot be undone so easily. Today, any time city dwellers or suburbanites want to invoke stereotypes of Appalachian people—or country people in general—as inbred brutes, the mention of *Deliverance* is enough.

"Let me tell you a story 'bout a man named Jed..."

a decade, building a loyal but small follow-ing. Then two things happened: sons Ronnie and Robbie started playing with the band (renamed the Del McCoury Band) on mandolin and banjo, respec-tively, and Nashville agent Lance LeRoy started representing the group just as he got word that his clients, the Johnson Mountain Boys, were disbanding.

Ronnie McCoury's Monroe-like mandolin playing has won the highest praise possible in the bluegrass world. Monroe, while sitting in with the McCoury unit once, removed his Stetson and put it on Ronnie's head, and the International Bluegrass Music Association named Ronnie mandolinist of the year in 1993 and 1994. In 1995, a year in which Monroe was also nominated, McCoury won again but told the awards-ceremony crowd that Monroe deserved it more, then walked into the audience and handed the plaque to Monroe. Robbie McCoury's driving but never dominating Scruggs-style banjo playing is another highlight of the McCoury Band's sound, which LeRoy has helped find a larger audience. With newcomer Jason Carter's twisting and sliding fiddle, Del's unmistakable voice, and a songbag that runs heavily to the blues, the band is right in the groove.

Hot Grass in Music City

The blues are a big part of the hottest band to come out of Nashville's lively bluegrass scene in recent years, named simply the Nashville Bluegrass Band. In 1984, banjo player Alan O'Bryant was offered the opportunity to take his band on the road, filling the bluegrass slot in a country music package tour. Unfortunately, his band had broken up, so he recruited guitarist Pat Enright, who had worked with Laurie Lewis in Phantoms of the Opry, mandolinist Mike Compton, and bass player Mark Hembree. The group decided to stay together after their nine-week hitch. The Nashville Bluegrass Band plumbs deeper for

The Nashville Bluegrass Band, more than many groups, highlights bluegrass' African American roots.

bluegrass' African-American connections than most bands. In addition to the blues, the band also does a cappella gospel singing in the style of black gospel groups such as the Fairfield Four, with whom they have collaborated. Like the Johnson Mountain Boys and the Dry Branch Fire Squad, the band also frequently presents songs as duets, with Enright usually leading and O'Bryant singing tenor. (Two-part arrangements leave more room for vocal improvisation than the usual three or four parts.) The band has remained relatively stable; former Kentucky Colonels member Roland White replaced Compton in 1989, Gene Libbea now handles the bass, and hot fiddler Stuart Duncan now plies his bow with the band.

Playing like Stuart Duncan is the ambition of the country's biggest bluegrass sensation, fiddler/singer Alison Krauss (b. 1971). With three Grammy awards, a platinum album, and a coveted slot on the Grand Ole Opry for her band Union Station, she could be a major-label mainstream country star in a nanosecond. But the former child prodigy from Decatur, Illinois, who sings like an angel and fiddles like the devil, continues to put bluegrass at the core of her music. She has sung harmony on a Linda Ronstadt record and played in huge arenas opening for country megastar Garth Brooks, but most of the music she makes with Union Station is bluegrass—not pure and not simple, but bluegrass nonetheless.

Bluegrass fans, always fearful for the survival of their music, are encouraged by the commercial success of Grammy-winner Alison Krauss (center) and her band, Union Station.

She and her bandmates represent bluegrass' third generation; they first heard the music on records of second-generation bands like Ricky Skaggs and Boone Creek, Doyle Lawson and Quicksilver, and J.D. Crowe and The New South, and only later found their way back to the Stanleys, Monroe, Flatt, and Scruggs. Two band members, mandolinist Adam Steffey and bassist Barry Bales, are products of the bluegrass program at East Tennessee University, which started in 1983 and is one of only two college-level bluegrass programs in the country. Another Alison, world-class banjo picker Alison Brown (b. 1961), a Harvard-educated former investment banker, played with Union Station for three years before moving on to more newgrass-oriented solo and studio work; she was replaced by the more than capable Ron Block.

Krauss disarms bluegrass purists who worry that success will go to her head: she says she won't play any more arenas (the boomy sound makes it impossible for the members of the band to hear each other). And she has spurned all major-label recording offers, remaining loyal to Rounder, the indie that first signed her at age fifteen, because the label allows the band to control their own recordings.

The Future

Alison Krauss' desire to keep control of her recordings is warranted, as the major labels don't really understand bluegrass. In search of a mass market for bluegrass in the 1960s, producers pushed drums and electric guitars and even got conservative Lester Flatt to record Bob Dylan's "Blowin' in the Wind." Their efforts ultimately failed to win mainstream acceptance of bluegrass and alienated the true believers. The majors have largely left bluegrass alone since 1976, when MCA dropped Jimmy Martin and the Osbornes, leaving Bill Monroe as the only bluegrass artist with a major-label contract.

Bluegrass loyalists will probably always worry about the future of their music: they are hopeful that increased exposure on the Opry and Nashville Network broadcasts will win new fans, yet remain suspicious that anyone who makes it big isn't really playing bluegrass. But bluegrass people have built institutions that help the music survive the ups and downs of musical fashion. *Bluegrass Unlimited*, a monthly magazine with a circulation of thirty thousand, keeps fans informed of the doings of established bands and rising newcomers at the same time serving as a forum for its highly opinionated readership. Several independent record labels specialize in bluegrass. Founded in 1985, The International Bluegrass Music Association promotes bluegrass on radio and television; runs a museum, hall of fame, and annual awards ceremony; and facilitates communication among musicians, promoters, deejays, and fans. And more than five hundred weekend festivals around the country and dozens more overseas have made it more possible for bluegrass musicians to make a living and provide opportunities for fans (many of whom are musicians themselves) to gather, swap tunes, hear new bands and old favorites, and renew the faith. With musicians who play for the love of it both pushing the limits of the music and digging deeper in the fertile soil of bluegrass roots, the future of bluegrass looks assured.

Recommended Reading

Cantwell, Robert. *Bluegrass Breakdown.* Urbana, Ill.: University of Illinois Press, 1984.

Clarke, Donald, ed. *The Penguin Encyclopedia of Popular Music.* London: Penguin Books, 1989.

Devan, Brett. "The Johnson Mountain Boys: The Number One Traditional Bluegrass Group in America." *Bluegrass Unlimited*, November 1987.

"Don Reno, 1926–1984." *Bluegrass Unlimited*, December 1984.

Godbey, Frank. Liner notes for Del McCoury's *A Deeper Shade of Blue* (Rounder).

Goldsmith, Thomas. "Alison Krauss and Union Station, 1995." *Bluegrass Unlimited*, June 1995.

Haney, F. Paul. "From the Women's Point of View." *Bluegrass Unlimited*, December 1989.

Henry, Murphy. "This Magic Moment: Owensboro, 1995." *Banjo Newsletter*, November 1995.

———. "Women in Bluegrass Music: A Seminar." *Bluegrass Unlimited*, December 1989.

Kelly, R.J. "Bill Keith: Sharing a Banjo Tightrope." *Bluegrass Unlimited*, January 1985.

Kochman, Marilyn, ed. *The Big Book of Bluegrass.* New York: Quill, 1984.

Liebling, Rachel. *High Lonesome: The Story of Bluegrass Music* (film). Northside Films, 1991.

Malone, Bill C. *Country Music USA.* Austin, Tex.: University of Texas Press, 1985.

———. *Southern Music, American Music.* Lexington, Ky.: University Press of Kentucky, 1979.

Menius, Art. "Dry Branch Fire Squad's Quest for Lonesome." *Bluegrass Unlimited*, July 1985.

———. "Finding the Roses Among the Brambles: The Lynn Morris Band." *Bluegrass Unlimited*, October 1993.

———. "The Nashville Bluegrass Band's American Lancao." *Bluegrass Unlimited*, October 1986.

Parsons, Penny. "The Nashville Bluegrass Band: Reaching for the Gold." *Bluegrass Unlimited*, July 1992.

———. "The Seldom Scene: All This and Fun, Too." *Bluegrass Unlimited*, December 1994.

Rinzler, Ralph. "Bill Monroe." *Stars of Country Music: Uncle Dave Macon to Johnny Rodriguez.* Urbana, Ill.: University of Illinois Press, 1975.

Rosenberg, Neil V. *Bluegrass: A History.* Urbana, Ill.: University of Illinois Press, 1985.

The Rounder Collective. Liner notes for the Bailey Brothers' *Have You Forgotten?* (Rounder).

Russell, Tony. *Blacks, Whites and Blues.* New York: Stein and Day, 1970.

Schoenberg, Mark. "A Thesis on the Evolution of Women in Bluegrass." *Bluegrass Unlimited*, April 1994.

Tribe, Ivan. Liner notes for the Lilly Brothers' *Country Songs* (Rounder).

Watson, Bruce. "This Here's All for Foot-Tappin' and Grin-Winnin'." *Smithsonian*, March 1993.

Wolfe, Charles K. Liner notes for *Altamont: Black String Band Music from the Library of Congress* (Rounder).

Recommended Listening

Berline, Byron. *Fiddle and a Song.* Sugar Hill.

The Bluegrass Album Band. *The Bluegrass Album.* Rounder.

———. *The Bluegrass Album, Volume 2.* Rounder.

The Country Gentlemen. *Country Songs Old and New.* Folkways.

Crowe, J.D. & the New South. *J.D. Crowe & The New South*. Rounder.

Dickens, Hazel. *By the Sweat of My Brow*. Rounder.

The Dillards. *Let It Fly*. Vanguard.

Dry Branch Fire Squad. *Just for the Record*. Rounder.

Flatt, Lester, and Earl Scruggs. *The Complete Mercury Sessions*. Mercury.

———. *The Golden Era (1950–1955)*. Rounder.

Grisman, David, Herb Pederson, and Jerry Garcia. *Home Is Where the Heart Is*. Rounder.

Hot Rize. *Take it Home*. Sugar Hill.

Jim & Jesse. *In the Tradition*. Rounder.

Johnson Mountain Boys. *Blue Diamond*. Rounder.

Krauss, Alison & Union Station. *Everytime You Say Goodbye*. Rounder.

Lawson, Doyle, and Quicksilver. *The Gospel Collection, Vol. 1*. Sugar Hill.

Lewis, Laurie, and Grant Street. *Singing My Troubles Away*. Flying Fish.

Martin, Jimmy. *You Don't Know My Mind*. Rounder.

McCoury, Del. *A Deeper Shade of Blue*. Rounder.

Monroe, Bill. *The Essential Bill Monroe & His Blue Grass Boys*. Columbia.

———. *Cryin' Holy Unto the Lord*. MCA.

Morris, Lynn. *The Lynn Morris Band*. Rounder.

Nashville Bluegrass Band. *Waitin' for the Hard Times to Go*. Sugar Hill.

New Grass Revival. *When the Storm Is Over/Fly Through the Country*. Flying Fish.

The Osborne Brothers. *Once More, Vols. 1 & 2*. Sugar Hill.

Reno, Don, and Red Smiley. *The Early Reno & Smiley*. King.

Rice, Tony. *Tony Rice Plays and Sings Bluegrass*. Rounder.

The Seldom Scene. *Act Four*. Sugar Hill.

Skaggs, Ricky, and Tony Rice. *Skaggs & Rice*. Sugar Hill.

The Stanley Brothers. *Angel Band*. Mercury.

Stanley, Ralph. *Saturday Night and Sunday Morning*. Freeland.

Trischka, Tony. *World Turning*. Rounder.

Watson, Doc. *Riding the Midnight Train*. Sugar Hill.

Wiseman, Mac. *Bluegrass Classics*. Rebel.

Various artists. *American Banjo Music Scruggs Style*. Folkways.

Various artists. *The Best of Bluegrass, Vol. 1: Standards*. Mercury.

Various artists. *The Great Dobro Sessions*. Sugar Hill.

Photography & Illustration Credits

AP/Wide World Photos: pp. 22–23, 40, 45

Archive Photos: pp. 12–13, 33, 54–55; Frank Driggs Collection: 9

© Maria Camillo: p. 24

Courtesy of Keith Case & Associates: © McGuire: pp. 53, 56–57; © Peter Nash: p. 58

Courtesy of Class Act Entertainment/© Hallmark Photography: p. 41 top

Corbis-Bettmann Archive: p. 10

Courtesy of Cash Edwards/© Irene Young: pp. 49, 50

Frank Driggs Collection: pp. 7, 16, 19, 20–21, 30, 35, 44, 46; Ray Flerlage: 31; Martin Wieser: 8

Everett Collection: pp. 32, 34; © Peter Nash: 47

Photofest: p. 36 left

Retna Ltd./© Beth Gwinn: p. 41 bottom

Showtime Archives: pp. 2, 11, 14, 17, 26, 27, 28, 29, 38, 39, 42, 48; Colin Escott: 18

UPI/Corbis-Bettmann: pp. 6, 36 right

Index